AMAZING ANIMALS

GIRAFFES

BY VALERIE
BODDEN

CREATIVE EDUCATION   CREATIVE PAPERBACKS

Published by Creative Education and
Creative Paperbacks
P.O. Box 227, Mankato, Minnesota 56002
Creative Education and Creative Paperbacks are
imprints of The Creative Company
www.thecreativecompany.us

Design by The Design Lab
Production by Angela Korte and Colin O'Dea
Art direction by Rita Marshall
Printed in the United States of America

Photographs by Alamy (WILDLIFE GmbH), Corbis
(Theo Allofs, Nigel J. Dennis/Gallo Images), Dream-
stime (Jenny Solomon), Getty Images (Suzi Eszterhas),
iStockphoto (2630ben, CJMGrafx, Enjoylife2, Dirk
Freder, emin kuliyev, Christian Musat, Thomas Polen,
Rick Wylie), Shutterstock (KrzysztofJ, Marni Rae
Photography)

Library of Congress Cataloging-in-Publication Data
Names: Bodden, Valerie, author.
Title: Giraffes / Valerie Bodden.
Series: Amazing animals.
Includes bibliographical references and index.
Summary: This revised edition surveys key aspects of
giraffes, describing the towering mammals' appear-
ance, behaviors, and habitats. A folk tale explains
why these creatures have long necks.
Identifiers: ISBN 978-1-64026-203-4 (hardcover)
/ ISBN 978-1-62832-766-3 (pbk) / ISBN 978-1-
64000-328-6 (eBook)
This title has been submitted for CIP processing under
LCCN 2019937909.

CCSS: RI.1.1, 2, 4, 5, 6, 7; RI.2.2, 5, 6, 7, 10;
RI.3.1, 5, 7, 8; RF.1.1, 3, 4; RF.2.3, 4

First Edition HC 9 8 7 6 5 4 3 2 1
First Edition PBK 9 8 7 6 5 4 3 2 1

Table of Contents

Long-Necked Mammals   4

Towering Animals   8

Giraffe Calves   15

Cooling Down   16

Roaming the Savannas   20

A Giraffe Tale   22

Read More   24

Websites   24

Index   24

Giraffes are the tallest animals on land. They have very long necks. They have long legs, too. If a giraffe stood next to a house, it could look in a second-floor window!

There are nine kinds of giraffes.

7

GIRAFFES

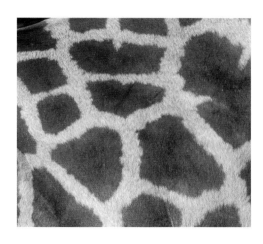

Giraffe spots are golden yellow to dark brown in color.

Giraffes have light yellow or white fur with darker spots. Each giraffe has its own **pattern** of spots. All giraffes have two bumps on top of their heads. These are called ossicones (*OSS-ih-kohns*).

pattern the way something is arranged

Giraffes are heavy animals. Adults weigh about as much as a car. Even though they weigh so much, giraffes can run fast. But they usually walk. Each foot is the size of a dinner plate!

Giraffes have the longest tails of any land animal.

Male giraffes are taller and heavier than females.

Giraffes live in Africa. Some giraffes live in forests. Others live on **savannas**. Giraffes' long necks allow them to see far across the land. They watch for predators like lions and hyenas.

savannas grassy areas with few trees

Giraffes

Giraffes eat leaves. They pull the leaves into their mouths with their strong tongues. Giraffes do not drink much water. They get most of the water they need from the leaves they eat. When they do drink, they must spread their front legs apart to reach the ground.

Giraffes' bluish-black tongues are about 21 inches (53.3 cm) long.

Mother giraffes watch over their calves for about 15 months.

A mother giraffe gives birth standing up. The **calf** falls to the ground. It is already as tall as a grown-up man. The calf can walk and run within a few hours of birth.

calf a baby giraffe

Fighting males will have less hair on their ossicones.

Giraffes live in **herds** called towers. About 10 giraffes are in a herd. Giraffes "talk" to each other with grunts, snorts, and moos. Male giraffes sometimes hit each other. They use their heads and necks to fight.

herds groups of animals that move around together

Giraffes spend most of their time eating. They do not sleep much. When they do sleep, it is for only a few minutes at a time. Giraffes usually sleep standing up.

Giraffes need only about two hours of sleep per day.

People around the world like to look at giraffes. Many zoos keep giraffes. Some people travel to Africa to see giraffes in the wild. It is fun to see these tall animals in person!

Giraffes can live for about 25 years in the wild.

A Giraffe Tale

People in Africa used to tell a story about why giraffes have long necks. They said Giraffe once looked like a deer. He ate grass. One year, the grass dried up. Giraffe was hungry. He wanted to eat the leaves on trees. He asked a magic man to make him tall. The man made Giraffe's neck and legs long. Then Giraffe could eat all the leaves he wanted!

Read More

Gagne, Tammy. *Giraffes*. Lake Elmo, Minn.: Focus Readers, 2018.

Hansen, Grace. *Giraffes*. Minneapolis: Abdo Kids, 2017.

Marsh, Laura. *Giraffes*. Washington, D.C.: National Geographic, 2016.

Websites

Enchanted Learning: Giraffes
https://www.enchantedlearning.com/themes/giraffe.shtml
This site has giraffe coloring pages, activities, and more.

National Geographic Kids: Giraffe
https://kids.nationalgeographic.com/animals/giraffe/
Learn more about the world's tallest animals.

San Diego Zoo Kids: Giraffe
https://kids.sandiegozoo.org/animals/giraffe
Learn more about the physical features of giraffes.

Note: Every effort has been made to ensure that the websites listed above are suitable for children, that they have educational value, and that they contain no inappropriate material. However, because of the nature of the Internet, it is impossible to guarantee that these sites will remain active indefinitely or that their contents will not be altered.

Index

Africa 11, 20

calves 15

food 12, 22

fur 7

herds 16

legs 4, 12, 22

necks 4, 11, 16, 22

ossicones 7

size 4, 8, 15

sleeping 19

sounds 16

threats 11

tongues 12

water 12